This book belongs to

Gifted by

On

LITTLE JAMAICANS©

CHEETAH TALE
THE COUNTRY OF DREARY

10 9 8 7 6 5 4 3 2 1

First published 2021 with an exclusive licence from the authors to CHEETAH® Purrrrrrr Publishing, an imprint of CHEETAH® Toys & More, LLC (CHEETAH®).

ISBN-13: 979-8-3304-0354-7
ISBN-10: 8-3304-0354-7

Contact information:

CHEETAH® Toys & More, LLC.
207 Main Street, 4th Floor
Hartford, CT 06016
USA

Port Antonio P.O.
Portland, Jamaica

info@mycheetahinc.com
paulettetrowers@yahoo.com
876-909-6311 (WHATSAPP ONLY)

Authors: Paulette Trowers, Juris Doctor, Fiona Porter-Lawson and Steven Doyle
Chief editor: Fiona Porter-Lawson
Illustrator: Wayne Powell
Audio: Story read by Maula Dunkley
Design: CHEETAH®

Your education begins with CHEETAH®.
Come with me. Let us learn about colours, how to get along with others, and so much more. You can also listen to our story online.
Ask your parents how.
Are you ready? Let's go! Let's go!

Once upon a time
in the country of Dreary,
there were only three colours
and this made the people weary.

King Black and Queen White
were bold and strong,
but young Prince Grey
and others couldn't get along.

The people were pale.
They all looked sad.
There was not much colour; it was very hard
to be glad.

Mother Nature knew
that this would not do.
So, she sent more colours;
a bright new crew.

Ruby Red was the first to come.
Red is the colour of love
and a very ripe plum.

He coloured sweet cherries
and apples that were just right.
He coloured them red
as he soared in flight.

Yummy Yellow came next to the dreary land.
Warm and bright, she came to give a hand.

Yellow is the colour of ripe bananas
and sunshine.
She called to Red, and he knew it was time.

8

So Red and Yellow worked very fast.
They mixed their colours well,
and there was a blast.

9

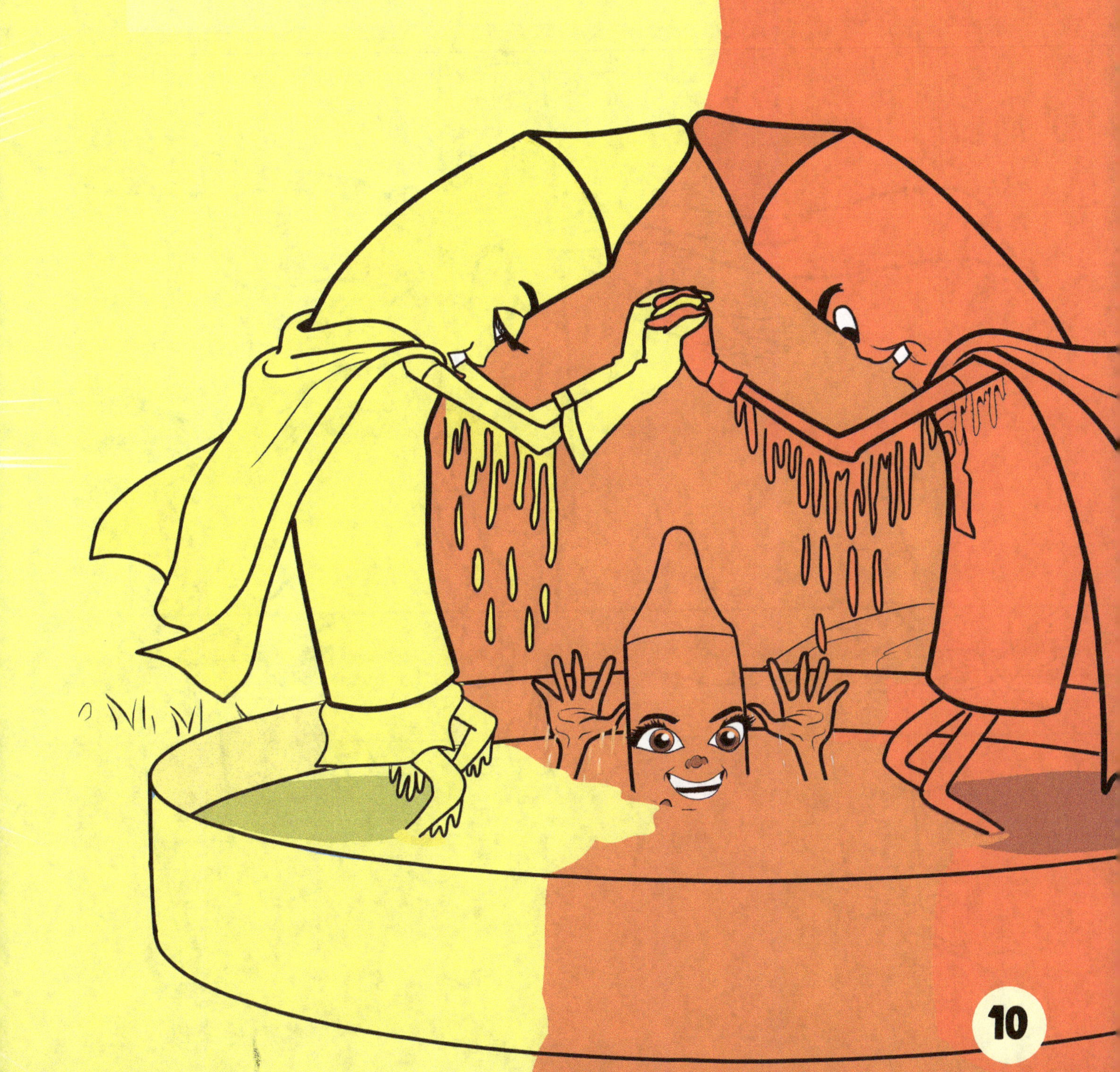

O
Y
R
11

They made Outstanding Orange
and lit up the sky.
Now three colours were
shining way up high.

But the land needed
more colours.
A few more would do.
Mother Nature then sent
Blazing Blue.

Blue gave the look of colours
to the sky and the sea.

She rode the waves.
She was as cool as could be.

R
O
B
Y

Blue and Yellow mixed their colours
to make Grand Green.
He was like nothing anyone had ever seen.

Green covered the grass and the leaves of the trees.
He spread over the hills,
making homes for birds and bees.

20

But Blue was not done. She called for radiant Red.
They talked and shared what was in their head.

21

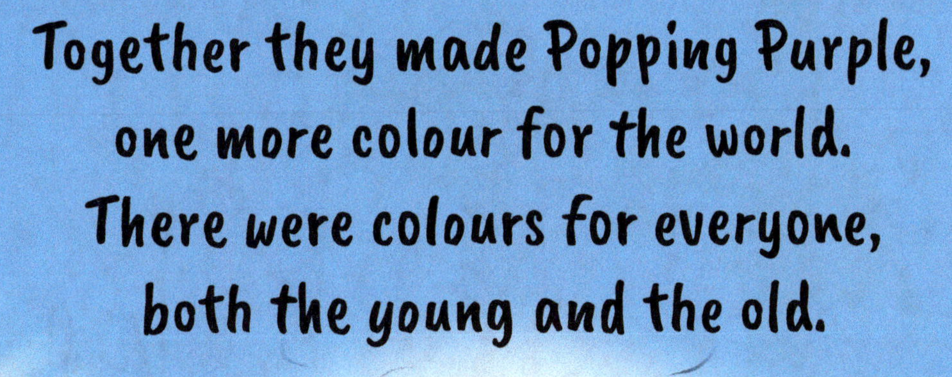

Together they made Popping Purple,
one more colour for the world.
There were colours for everyone,
both the young and the old.

Y
G
O
R
23

Purple coloured some berries and grapes as they grew.
He splashed his pretty colour on many flowers too.

The people of the country looked on in awe.
They could not believe all the colours they saw.

But Black, White and Grey
had ruled for so long.
They thought these new colours
did not belong.

Their family came, all shades of black
and grey and told the bright
new colours to go away.

But the bright colours were there to stay.
So, they argued and
fussed for most of the day.

29

Black, White and Grey stomped their feet;
each with a frown.
They grew very angry;
no one wanted to back down.

The bright colours thought the royals were bleak,
and made the people sad all days of the week.

They thought Black, White and Grey's
behaviour was wrong,
but these royals were oh so very strong.

P
O
G
R
B
C
C
32

So, the bright colours came together
and made a plan.
They would create even more colours on the land.

They mixed and blended
and made new colours,
Brave Brown, Interesting Indigo,
Vibrant Violet and others.

B

Soon all the colours
began to fight.
Every colour fought
with all their might.
35

36

They had weapons of silver and
weapons of gold.
They would not back down.
They were all so bold.
37

But Black, White and Grey
would not leave,
for they had a sneaky
trick up their sleeve.

40

G
41

The battle was noisy,
and the bright colours were chased away.
Was the fight lost?
Was it done for the day?

The people of Dreary wanted to help out.
They gave a wail and
called for the colours in a great shout.

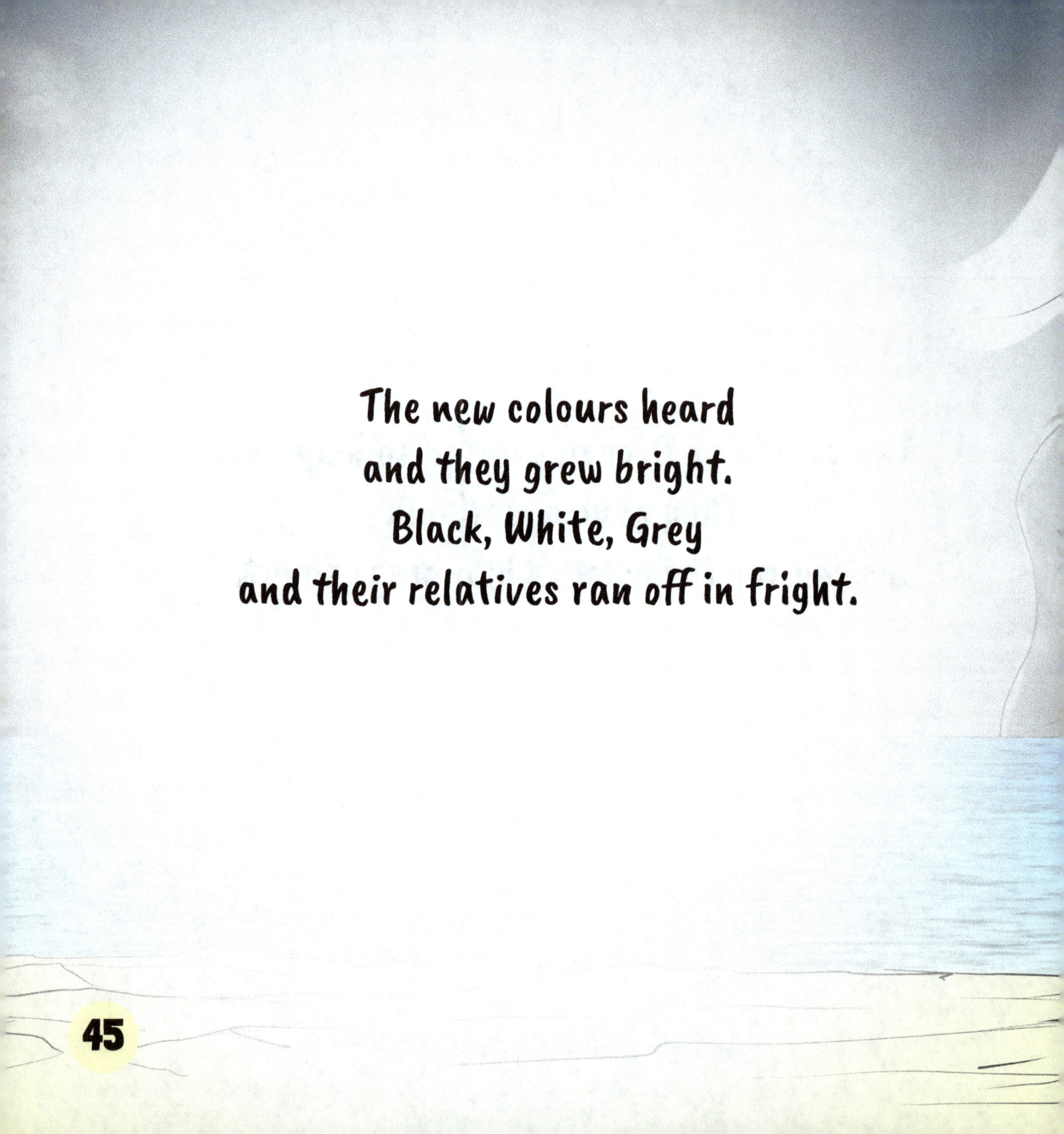

The new colours heard
and they grew bright.
Black, White, Grey
and their relatives ran off in fright.

46

47

The people had saved the new colours
in the country of Dreary.
Everyone was happy and oh, so cheery.

The colours then made a rainbow up high.

When a day was rainy,
it would brighten the sky.

Yet, Mother Nature knew all was not right.
The land needed all the colours,
not just the brights.

51

She brought back the blacks, whites and greys.
Now, all the colours would be there always!

52

So, she told everyone
that they should not fight,
no matter their colour,
dark, pale or bright.

The colours said 'sorry'; every single one.
They were sorry for fighting and
all the bad things they had done.

They promised not to argue; they would all be friends.
Together they would make lots of colourful blends.

56

R
P
W

Red worked with White
and made Pretty Pink.
The colours were happy,
more than you would think.

P
G
R
B
W
W
59

With all the colours working together,
the country was alive.
It was a place where things of every colour could thrive.

Mother Nature gave crayons
to the girls and boys.
Now they could add colours to their books and little toys.

The colours showed them what to do,
and Dreary became a new land for me and for you.

Country of Dreary Jingle

A promise from nature, the rainbow in the sky.

All of the colours looking down from up high.

red, orange, yellow, green, and blue,

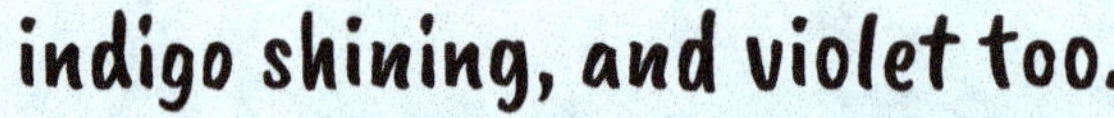

indigo shining, and violet too.

All working together in this great land.

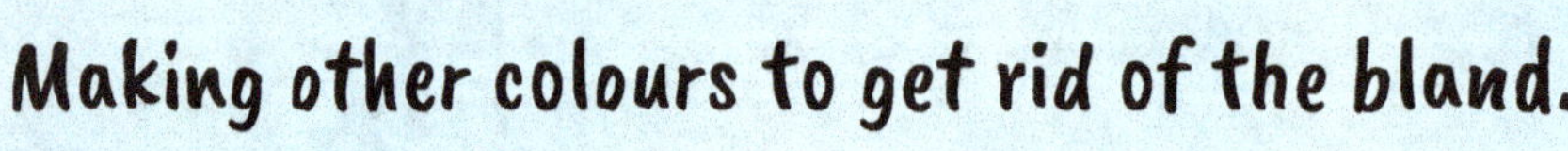

Making other colours to get rid of the bland.

From the tallest mountain to the deepest sea.

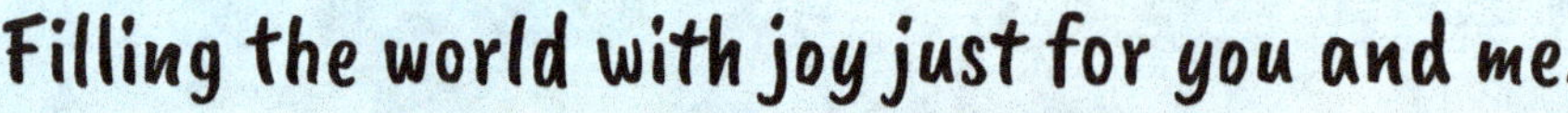

Filling the world with joy just for you and me.

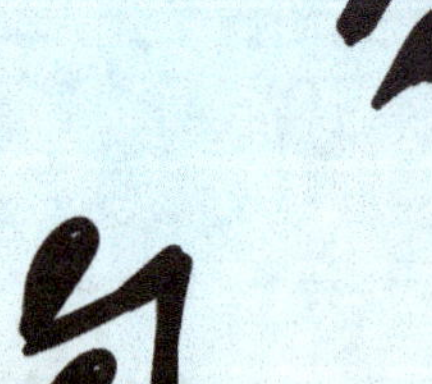

Did you enjoy the story?
Ready to read it again?
Let's go! Let's go!

An activity

Mixing colour

Use the pictures below to complete the next activity.

Orange

Green

Pink

Purple

Colour the crayons to complete the mixing.

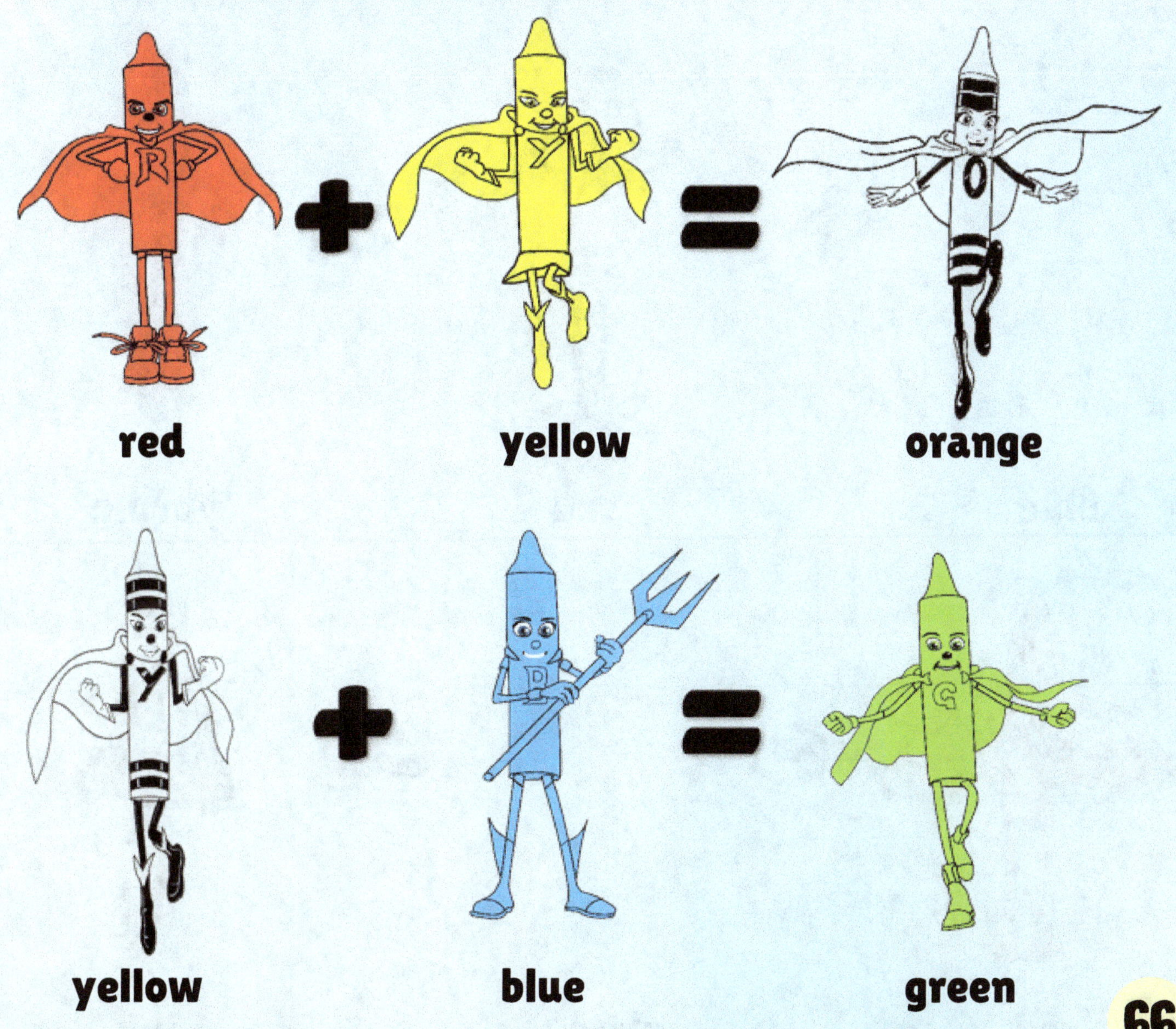

colour the crayons to complete the mixing.

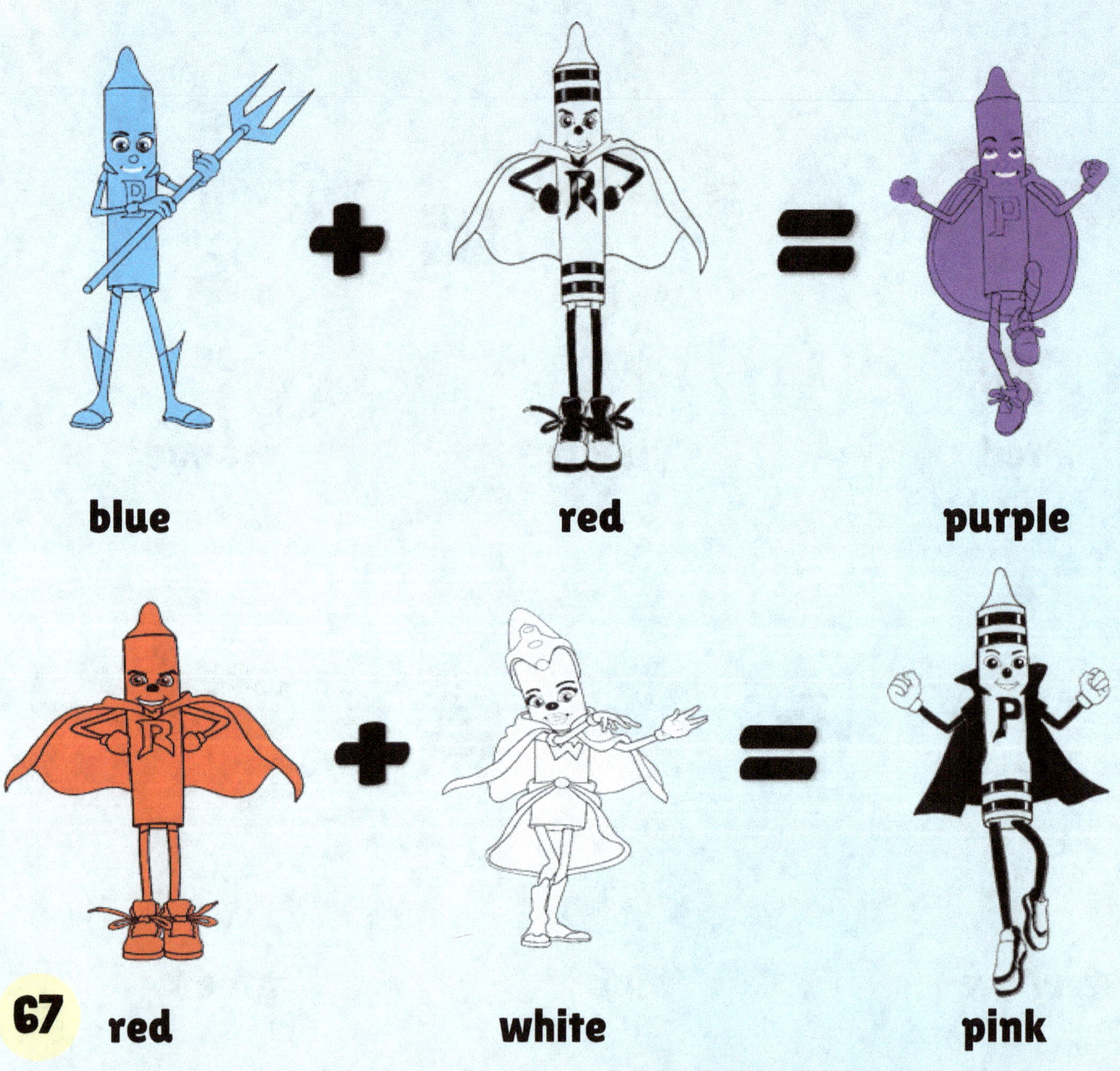

CHEETAH® CREW

Thanks to the following members of the CHEETAH® crew who reviewed,
critiqued and contributed to this book:
Taneisha Dawkins
Steven Doyle
Fiona Porter-Lawson
Rosemarie Pottinger
Feri Setiawan
Kimona Smith
Janice Trowers
Karen Wilson

68

black
white
grey
brown
red
purple

orange
yellow
indigo
green
blue
pink
violet